Butterfly Eggs

by Helen Frost

Consulting Editor: Gail Saunders-Smith, Ph.D.

Consultant: Dr. Ronald L. Rutowski,
Professor of Biology, Arizona State University

Pebble Books

an imprint of Capstone Press
Mankato, Minnesota

Pebble Books are published by Capstone Press
151 Good Counsel Drive, P.O. Box 669, Mankato, Minnesota 56002
http://www.capstone-press.com

2 3 4 5 6 07 06 05 04 03 02

Library of Congress Cataloging-in-Publication Data
Frost, Helen, 1949–
    Butterfly eggs/by Helen Frost.
    p. cm.—(Butterflies)
    Includes bibliographical references and index.
    Summary: A simple introduction to where and how butterflies lay their eggs.
    ISBN 0-7368-0227-4
    1. Butterflies—Eggs—Juvenile literature. [1. Butterflies—Eggs. 2. Butterflies—
Habits and behavior.] I. Title. II. Series: Frost, Helen, 1949– Butterflies.
QL544.2.F765 1999
595.78´91468—dc21   98-44902
                                                                                CIP
                                                                                 AC

Note to Parents and Teachers

The Butterflies series supports national science standards related to
the diversity and unity of life. This book describes where butterflies
lay eggs and the appearance of butterfly eggs. The photographs
support early readers in understanding the text. The repetition of
words and phrases helps early readers learn new words. This book
also introduces early readers to subject-specific vocabulary words,
which are defined in the Words to Know section. Early readers
may need assistance to read some words and to use the Table
of Contents, Words to Know, Read More, Internet Sites, and
Index/Word List sections of the book.

Table of Contents

4

Female butterflies
lay eggs.

bordered patch on common sunflower

6

Each kind of butterfly
lays eggs on a different
kind of plant.

anise swallowtail on Queen Anne's lace

8

Some butterflies lay one egg on a plant.

clouded sulphur egg on clover

Some butterflies lay many eggs on a plant.

tawny emperor eggs on hackberry tree

12

Some butterfly eggs
are smooth.

black swallowtail egg on Queen Anne's lace

13

14

Some butterfly eggs
are bumpy.

gulf fritillary eggs on passionflower plant

Some butterfly eggs
are green.

malachite eggs on ruellia plant

18

Some butterfly eggs
are red.

guava skipper egg on guava plant

20

Caterpillars hatch
from butterfly eggs.

monarch caterpillar on milkweed plant

Words to Know

bumpy—having round lumps

caterpillar—a wormlike animal that changes into a butterfly; caterpillars hatch from butterfly eggs.

female—an animal that can give birth or lay eggs; female butterflies lay eggs.

hatch—to break out of an egg; caterpillars hatch from butterfly eggs.

smooth—even and free from bumps

Read More

Burton, Jane. *Egg: A Photographic Story of Hatching.* New York: Dorling Kindersley, 1994.

Hamilton, K. R. *The Butterfly Book: A Kid's Guide to Attracting, Raising, and Keeping Butterflies.* Santa Fe, N.M.: John Muir Publications, 1997.

Norsgaard, E. Jaediker. *Butterflies: Butterfly Magic for Kids.* Animal Magic for Kids. Milwaukee: Gareth Stevens Publishing, 1996.

Saunders-Smith, Gail. *Butterflies.* Animals: Life Cycles. Mankato, Minn.: Pebble Books, 1997.

Internet Sites

Egg Anatomy
http://www.EnchantedLearning.com/subjects/ butterfly/anatomy/Egg.shtml

Monarch Watch—Biology
http://www.monarchwatch.org/biology/index.htm

Where Do Butterflies Come From?
http://www.hhmi.org/coolscience/butterfly

Index/Word List

Word Count: 57
Early-Intervention Level: 10

Editorial Credits

Colleen Sexton, editor; Steve Christensen, cover designer; Kimberly Danger and
   Sheri Gosewisch, photo researchers

Photo Credits

Charles W. Melton, 18
Colephoto/Robin Cole, 14
David Liebman, 10
Fred Siskind, 8
Jay Ireland & Georgienne Bradley, cover
Jeffrey Glassberg, 4
Photophile, 6
Robert McCaw, 12
Root Resources/C. Postmus, 16
Stuart Wilson, 20
Visuals Unlimited/Leroy Simon, 1